American Women
at War™

WOMEN SOLDIERS, SPIES, AND PATRIOTS OF THE AMERICAN REVOLUTION

MARTHA KNEIB

The Rosen Publishing Group, Inc., New York

To Candy Lake, the best partner in crime one could hope for

Published in 2004 by The Rosen Publishing Group, Inc.
29 East 21st Street, New York, NY 10010

Library of Congress Cataloging-in-Publication Data

Kneib, Martha.
Women soldiers, spies, and patriots of the American Revolution/Martha Kneib.—1st ed.
    v. cm.—(American women at war)
Includes bibliographical references and index.
Contents: Deborah Samson—Nancy Hart—Lydia Darragh—Mercy Otis Warren—Esther DeBerdt Reed—Elizabeth Martin—Sybil Ludington—Margaret Corbin—After the war.
ISBN 0-8239-4454-9 (lib. bdg.)
1. Women soldier—United States—Biography—Juvenile literature.
2. Women spies—United States—Biography—Juvenile literature.
3. Women revolutionaries—United States—Biography—Juvenile literature. 4. United States—History--Revolution, 1775-1783—Participation, Female—Juvenile literature. 5. United States—History—Revolution, 1775-1783—Secret service—Juvenile literature.
6. United States—History—Revolution, 1775-1783—Women—Juvenile literature. [1. United States—History—Revolution, 1775-1783—Women. 2. Women—Biography.]
I. Title. II. Series.
E276.K58 2004
973.3'092'2—dc22

                                                                2003016924

Manufactured in the United States of America

On the front cover: "Molly Pitcher" (Mary Ludwig Hays McCauly, 1754-1832) takes her husband's place as he lies wounded, and prepares to fire a cannon at the British during the American Revolution.
On the back cover: a thirteen star American Revolutionary flag

Contents

INTRODUCTION

In 1764, Great Britain was facing bankruptcy due to the expense of the French and Indian War. In a quest to find new sources of revenue, British prime minister George Grenville turned his eye toward the American colonies. The war had been fought on their soil, and the colonies had benefited from it; therefore, it seemed proper to him that they pay the expense.

The American colonists, however, did not think that the British Parliament had the right to tax them. With few exceptions, the colonies were self-governing, with royally appointed officials working with colonial legislatures. Many British officials, including Lord George Germain, made their opinions known about the growing discontent in the American colonies. During a debate in Parliament on March 28, 1774, Germain said "nor can I think he will do a better thing than to put an end to their town meetings. I would not have men of a mercantile cast every day collecting themselves together and debating about political matters. . ."[1]

Parliament had not been in the habit of interfering with the colonies' policies of self-government. In Virginia, Richard Bland declared that the colony's legislature had the right to enact "laws for the internal government of the colony," while in "our external government we are and must be subject to the authority of the British Parliament." However, he was clear that taxation rested safely within that authority. "Any tax respecting our internal [policy] which may hereafter be imposed on us by act of Parliament is arbitrary, as depriving us of our rights, and may be opposed."[2]

Parliament began in 1764 with the Sugar Act and the Currency Act. No outward signs of rebellion

Hundreds of infuriated Americans protest the Stamp Act of 1765 in this drawing. Fifty-four types of documents were listed as taxable under the law. This included marriage licenses, deeds, and receipts. The British expected a good deal of grumbling from the colonies but were not prepared for some of the massive rallies that were incited by American newspapers, who were adversely affected by the law.

were prompted by these two acts, but when Parliament passed the Stamp Act in October 1765, the die was cast. The Stamp Act required that taxes be paid on all printed materials like newspapers and legal documents—even playing cards! Christopher Gadsden of Charleston, South Carolina, wrote that Parliament must think of the Americans as "tame apes" if it thought they would submit to "such a hateful, baneful expedient."[3]

Across the colonies, small groups of citizens began to take action. Officials were burnt in effigy, their property was vandalized, and some were tarred and feathered. At least one was killed. Violence against officials became so common, the *New York Gazette* even asked in one article "whether it would not be prudent for all Stamp Officers to insure their houses."[4]

In the end, Georgia was the only colony to attempt to uphold the Stamp Act. (The act was quickly repealed, but other acts of Parliament like the Townshend Acts of 1767 and the Intolerable Acts of 1774 [the Quartering Act, the Quebec Act, the Massachusetts Government Act, the Administration of Justice Act, and the Boston Port Act] followed.) Colonial legislators began to make their protests more official. One form of protest they had in mind—a boycott of British goods— could be very effective if enough people would cooperate. The people who had to be receptive to the idea were not just men, but also women, because they were the ones who normally pur- chased British goods like wool, tea, and candles. If the state legislatures wanted to be successful with their boycott, women had to be enlisted to the cause.

Caleb Bingham, a nineteenth-century writer
for *The American Preceptor*, wrote in 1811 that,
"Needlework, the care of domestic affairs, and a
serious and retired life, is the proper function of
women."[5] Prior to the Revolutionary War, most
people, including most women, would have agreed
with this sentiment. Men's and women's lives
rarely overlapped. Men were responsible for plow-
ing fields, harvesting, and conducting business
dealings and financial transactions. Women's
responsibilities were often relegated to traditional
household chores and for bearing and raising children. For most people of this time, this was the
proper and desirable way for adults to behave.

A young girl growing up before the war would
have helped her mother around the house as much
as possible. She would have first been assigned sim-
ple tasks. By the time she was eight or nine years of
age, she would spend long hours spinning wool and
taking care of her younger siblings. She might have
been taught to read so that she could read her Bible,
but she would not have been educated like her
brothers would have been. Her mother would be
responsible for teaching her all she needed to know.

When a young woman was ready to marry, she
would depend on her parents to choose her husband.

Many young women were quite frightened by the prospect of marriage because if there were problems, divorces were difficult to obtain. If a man turned out to be cruel, for instance, the young woman would have little option but to remain with him. Elizabeth Smith Shaw wrote in a letter in 1786 that girls approached marriage with "the most fearful apprehensions—as it is the [most] important crisis upon

A cartoon depicts a typical colonial household in early eighteenth-century America. The father is seen reclining with a pipe while the women in the family prepare a meal and make clothing. At the time, women and men tended to have separate roles and responsibilities in the family.

which our fate depends."[6] Although apprehensive, girls would rather marry than not, as single women were looked down upon. One newspaper columnist of the time described unmarried women as "good-for-nothing creatures."[7] After marriage, a woman was expected to take care of household duties first and foremost—as William Livingston put it, to be happy "in their chimney corners."[8] The restrictions that bounded the lives of women were very real. The few women who did not marry were often without a means of financial support. This need to survive prompted many women into unwelcome relationships.

Benjamin Franklin encouraged men to discuss financial matters with their wives, but few did so. In fact, during the war, many women whose husbands served in the army discovered that they had little idea about how to run the family farm. They did not know how to plow, when to plant, when to harvest, or how much their crops were worth. Widows found out the hard way that they knew little about the value of their houses or land and did not know about debts their husbands owed or even how much money their husbands had earned before the war. Financial ignorance cost many families during and after the war as women were preyed upon. Many women were offered much less money than their crops or lands were worth. Other women tried to run their husbands' businesses only to discover that their business partners kept important papers and other information from them.

But as the men left home to fight, women were increasingly left in charge. Most women in these unfamiliar positions soon learned how to attend to their new duties. One such woman was Thomas Jefferson's mother, a very skilled businesswoman, who learned how to manage business affairs after her first husband died.

Many women supported the fight for independence, even though it meant that they had to make personal sacrifices. Most would have agreed with an anonymous Philadelphia woman, who wrote to a British officer, "My only brother I have sent to the camp, with my prayers and blessings. I have retrenched every superfluous expense in my table and family; tea I have not drunk since last Christmas, nor bought a new cap or gown since your defeat at Lexington; and what I never did before, have learned to knit, making stockings of American wool, and this way do I throw in my mite for the public good . . . I have the pleasure to assure you that these are the sentiments of all my sister Americans."[9]

Aiding the war effort by engaging in activities at home or by doing the tasks normally left to men was not enough for some women. After the men rode off to war, these women engaged in heroic efforts to help make America independent.

DEBORAH SAMSON

Deborah Samson wished to take a dynamic role in the Revolutionary War. In order to be eligible for active duty, she was forced to dress as a man and enlist in the army under a male name. Most women who did this were never discovered. Some we know only by name today. At least one woman died on the battlefield. Another rose to the rank of sergeant before being discovered and then dismissed. It might seem strange today, but when revealed, women like Samson were

Deborah Samson is pictured here in typical neoclassic dress in this portrait from 1797. Neoclassicism was a European cultural movement that looked to ancient Greece and Rome for inspiration in philosophy, art, and even fashion. Democracy was one of the ancient ideas revived by the neoclassicists.

the focus of ridicule and derision. Because of this, we know almost nothing about most of them. After the Revolutionary War, women normally did not talk about their experiences. However, Samson spoke openly of her role in the war.

Once she decided to enlist, Samson used the name "Timothy Thayer." But as she signed the enlistment papers, someone she knew spotted her and her deception was exposed. The recruiters were furious. They tore up Samson's enlistment papers and shouted at her to go home and behave like a proper woman. They threatened to punish her severely if she tried to enlist again.

Samson could not be frightened away by angry recruiters. In fact, her entire life had been one of hardship, so the prospect of serving in the army must have seemed more like an adventure than something potentially dangerous. Her friends described her as fearless. "It cannot be denied that this romantic girl exhibited something of the same spirit as Joan of Arc [who] felt herself inspired with resolution to go forth and do battle in her country's cause . . . "[1] Like Joan of Arc, the fifteenth-century woman who led troops against a British invasion of France in 1429, Samson felt as if she had also been called to defend her country against the British.

Samson was the eldest child of six children born in Plympton, Massachusetts, to Jonathan Samson and Deborah Bradford Samson. They were a poor couple who could not provide for their family. The situation worsened when Samson's father left home for an expedition at sea and never returned. Samson's mother was now so desperate that authorities removed the children from the home and placed them elsewhere. Deborah was separated from her siblings and placed in the care of a distant relative. Three years, later, when her guardian died, she was placed in the home of a farmer living in Middleborough, Massachusetts. She was now ten years old and was expected to work as an indentured servant.

As a servant, Samson could not go to school. She listened instead to the lessons of others and borrowed the books of neighboring children. By working independently, she eventually learned to read and write.

When she was eighteen years of age, Samson was free of her indenture, and she left the farm to find work in nearby Bellingham. One of the first things she did was acquire an education. Within a few months, she had so greatly increased her knowledge that she was better educated than children who had attended school for years.

After hostilities broke out, Samson enthusiastically supported the war effort and plotted how she might serve in the army to fight for her country. Samson had managed to save twelve dollars from a job with the local school, and she used it to purchase the cloth she would need for her disguise. As she completed each piece, she hid it in a haystack. Upon finishing the uniform, she announced to everyone that she was leaving the area to seek better wages. Instead, Samson went only as far as the woods of Bellingham so she could change into her disguise. Although discovered the first time, the second time, in October 1782, she managed to enlist as "Robert Shurtleff" and was enrolled for the entire length of the war. She was a volunteer in the Fourth Massachusetts Regiment, led by Captain Nathan Thayer.

Because she had grown up doing heavy labor on a farm, Samson was well suited to this life of pretense as a man. She was strong enough to pass for a teenage boy and could keep pace with the men of the company. She had no problems marching or firing her musket.

Samson's first test came when the company men were given uniforms. Because hers did not fit, she simply took out needle and thread and altered it herself. When the company commander's wife commented that it was

This illustration depicts the style of uniform worn by soldiers in the Continental army. Deborah Samson would have worn a similar uniform when she fought the British disguised as a man.

strange for a boy to know so much about sewing, Samson responded quickly. She said that her mother had been a seamstress, and as she had no sisters, she had been required to learn sewing to help her mother with her work. The explanation worked and no more questions were asked.

For three years, Samson led the life of a soldier. She fought in battles and endured hardships so courageously that she was commended by other men in her company and by her officers. Although they sometimes teased her by calling her "Molly" due to her beardlessness, the soldiers assumed she was a teenage boy too young to shave.

Soldiers in the Revolutionary War were badly paid as well as poorly fed. Money from Congress came slowly or not at all. Because roads were often impassable due to rain or snow, supply wagons of food often could not get to hungry troops. Many soldiers did not have shoes or blankets. Private Joseph Plumb Martin, who wrote an account of his war experiences, described many instances in which he nearly froze to death on cold nights or suffered exposure due to sleeping outside in pouring rain. "I was faint," he wrote, "having slept but very little the preceding night, nor had I eaten a mouthful of victuals for more than twenty-four hours. I waddled on as well and as fast as I could."[2]

Samson was familiar with hunger and long cold nights without a blanket. She persevered as bravely as the rest of her troop. Although she was wounded several times, sources disagree on the number and placement of her injuries. She was said to have had a sword cut to the head and then, four months later, been hit by a bullet that went through her shoulder. Other sources insist it was her thigh that was hit and that she hid in the woods until it healed. Because she was hiding her identity, she sought no medical treatment.

Three years after she enlisted, Samson's company was in Philadelphia when she became sick with what was then called "brain fever." Many soldiers had fallen ill with the same symptoms, and many had died. At first, Samson tried to hide the fact she was sick. She did not want to be taken to the hospital where her secret identity would undoubtedly be exposed. Eventually, she grew so ill that she was carried to the hospital and left there. At the time of her arrival, her condition was considered hopeless. At that time, patients in such a grave state were not well attended.

The drawing above shows Deborah Samson handing a letter to General George Washington. After Samson was discharged from the military, she continued to live a life contrary to societal norms. During her life and even more so after her death, she achieved legendary status as the first recognized American female soldier. Today, she is known as the official heroine of the state of Massachusetts.

One day the attending physician, Dr. Barnabas Binney, walked by and asked how the young man in the bed was progressing. He was told that the man had died. The doctor felt for a pulse and, finding one, tried to place his hand on the man's heart. When he did so, he discovered that his male patient was a woman with her breasts bound to her chest by bandages.

The doctor did not immediately reveal Samson's secret. Instead, Samson was given the best treatment the hospital could offer, and when she had recovered enough to be moved, the doctor took her into his own house. The doctor's niece was smitten by the brave young soldier. The doctor, however, did not tell his niece what he knew about the soldier called Robert Shurtleff. Fortunately, Samson found a way to discourage the young girl's attraction without revealing herself.

When Samson had fully recovered from the fever, Dr. Binney went to her commanding officer. The commanding officer then ordered Samson to carry a letter to General George Washington. She was by now certain her secret was out.

Samson delivered the order to Washington with trepidation, sure that she had been discovered and would be punished. But Washington, upon reading the letter, prepared an honorable discharge for her. He also gave her a small sum of money, enough to pay her expenses back home.

Samson changed back into female attire and returned to Massachusetts. After the war ended, she married Benjamin Gannett in 1784, and they had three children: Earl, Mary, and Patience. Although she kept busy on the farm with her husband, Samson also took the time to give lectures about her war experiences. After much protest in 1792, she was given back pay the army had previously withheld from her. By 1805, Congress voted that she should receive a war veteran's pension.

Today, there is a monument to Deborah Samson in Plympton, Massachusetts, and another monument marks her grave at Rock Ridge Cemetery, in the nearby town of Sharon.

NANCY MORGAN HART

One of Georgia's most colorful and heroic patriots of the Revolutionary War was Nancy Morgan Hart, a six-foot-tall, cross-eyed, rather plain redhead with smallpox scars on her face who had a penchant for cursing.

Little is known of Hart's early life. Sources disagree on the year of her birth. Some historians say 1735, while others claim it to be either 1744 or 1747. Hart's birthplace is also unknown; it was probably either Pennsylvania or

North Carolina. In the eighteenth century, people didn't necessarily keep records of the place and time of their birth unless they were from upper-class families. Nancy Morgan married Benjamin Hart sometime around 1755, and they moved to northern Georgia in 1771. There, Hart, a flame-haired sharp-shooter, made an immediate impression on the locals, so much so that local Native Americans called the creek by her house "War Woman Creek."[1]

By the time the war broke out, Hart, who was described as "a honey of a patriot, but the devil of a wife"[2] had eight children to raise. Together with her husband she helped farm more than 400 acres (162 hectares) in the Broad River settlement in Georgia. Despite the difficulty of raising eight children while acting as community midwife and pharmacist, Hart helped her husband with the farm and also hunted for wild game.

Hart thoroughly supported the fight for independence. Her husband, whom she described as a "poor stick,"[3] was less enthusiastic than she. Hart was so zealous that she reportedly undertook dangerous tasks to help the patriot cause. According to various legends, she infiltrated British camps sometimes acting like a half-wit, sometimes disguised as a man. She listened to the conversations and then reported back to patriot units. On one occasion, she went out with a basket of eggs to sell to the British and was so successful at eavesdropping that she was able to gather extremely valuable intelligence. By supporting the patriot cause and spying, Hart eventually became well known to British sympathizers in the area.

The deed that propelled Hart from occasional spy to beloved heroine of colonial Georgia happened in Hart's own home. Her husband was

In this engraving, an American woman serves tea to a British officer while attempting to get information from him. Because Americans were expected to entertain the British soldiers, they often had excellent access to information about British military plans.

working in the fields far away from the house, leaving Hart and their thirteen-year-old daughter Sukey alone at the little log cabin. Five or six Loyalists (sources disagree on a number) from the British camp in Augusta arrived at the cabin and demanded to be fed. They knew about the red-headed, loudmouthed woman who let everyone know how she felt about the British, and they wanted to make trouble for her.

At first, Hart adamantly refused to feed the men. She pointed out that she had only one turkey, and it was old. But the Loyalists were determined to give her as much trouble as possible. One of them shot the turkey and insisted again that Hart feed the men.

Although she was very angry, Hart began cooking. If the men were well fed they might go away without harming her or Sukey. But as their dinner was being prepared, they began bragging about how they had just killed Colonel John Dooley in his bed. Dooley was a friend and neighbor of Hart's, and she was outraged by this act of violence. At that point her plan changed from simply feeding the men and hoping they would go away to plotting their capture and death.

Hart began setting out the food and drink. She made sure the Loyalists had plenty of whiskey and entertained them with humorous stories. On the pretext of needing more spring water, she sent her daughter out of the house to raise the alarm. Hart and her neighbors had hidden a conch shell by the well and had arranged for everyone to know how to blow a signal if an emergency arose. Sukey fetched the water, but she also blew the conch shell and alerted her father and their neighbors to the situation at home.

Nancy Morgan Hart is pictured above holding the uninvited Loyalists at gunpoint. Loyalists were also referred to as Tories, after their affiliation with the Tory political party. During the eighteenth century, the Tories were mainly concerned with entrusting the king with total rule. Today, the term "Tory" is used as a nickname for England's Conservative Party.

When Sukey returned, Hart began passing the men's muskets outside to her through a hole in the log cabin wall. She had gotten three muskets outside the house before the men noticed what she was doing. They immediately rushed at her, but Hart picked up one of the muskets and pointed it at the men, who stopped.

This standoff continued for a few moments until one of the men reached for a gun. Hart shot him, dropped the single-shot weapon, and grabbed another musket that Sukey had passed back into the house. A second man moved, and Hart shot him as well. The first man died immediately, but the second was merely injured.

At this point, Benjamin Hart arrived with the neighbors to find his wife holding off the remaining Loyalists with another musket. Hart explained that these were the men who had killed Colonel Dooley. The neighbors wanted to shoot the Loyalists for committing such a terrible crime, but Hart argued that "shooting's too good for them."[4] Instead, the prisoners were marched out to the forest and hanged.

After the war, the Hart family moved to Brunswick, Georgia, where Benjamin Hart died. Later, Nancy Hart moved to Kentucky with one of her children, where she died in 1830.

For her courage and resourcefulness, Hart became one of Georgia's most famous heroines. Hart County was named for her, as were the Nancy Hart Highway and the Nancy Hart Historical Park. Two memorials to her deeds have been erected in Hartwell, Georgia. In 1997, she was honored as a Georgia Woman of Achievement.

In 1912, six well-preserved skeletons were unearthed within a half-mile of the site of the Hart cabin. It cannot be proved, but many people believe these are the remains of the Loyalists who killed Colonel Dooley and then made the mistake of getting on the wrong side of Nancy Morgan Hart.

LYDIA DARRAGH

War has a way of forcing people to make hard decisions. Such was the lot of Lydia Darragh of Philadelphia. Darragh belonged to the Society of Friends (Quakers), a religion that had been brought to the colonies from Great Britain to flee persecution. Quakers bar members from engaging in acts of war or violence for any reason. This policy of pacifism is echoed in their official declaration:

> We feel bound explicitly to avow our un-
> shaken persuasion that all

war is utterly incompatible with the plain precepts of our divine Lord and Law-giver, and the whole spirit of His Gospel, and that no plea of necessity or policy, however urgent or peculiar, can avail to release either individuals or nations from the paramount allegiance which they owe to Him who hath said, "Love your enemies."[1]

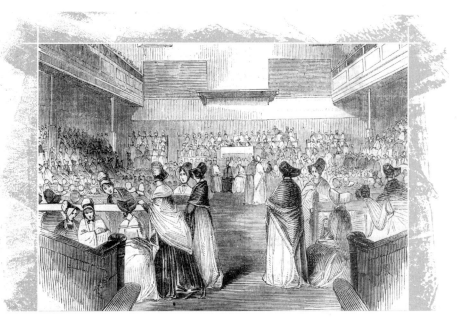

Quakers gather together for their annual meeting. The Quakers elected no official minister to lead their congregations. Instead, their sermons were open forums for all members, including women, wanting to profess their spiritual thoughts to fellow believers. The Quaker philosophy of equality was very progressive for the time period.

The allure of belonging to a religion that preached tolerance, equality, and peace was undeniable. Many Quakers left Great Britain for the colonies, including William Penn, who founded the colony of Pennsylvania. In that colony, Quakers were welcomed and found a new home free from persecution.

Darragh herself had been born in Dublin, Ireland, in 1729. She married William Darragh, a teacher, in 1753. Shortly thereafter, the couple moved across the sea to Philadelphia, where they lived in the company of other Quakers. Because her husband made very little money as a teacher, Lydia Darragh brought in most of the family's income through her various jobs as nurse, midwife, and undertaker. The couple had nine children, though only four survived.

During the early days of the war, Darragh was not involved with the war effort. To do so would be to put herself at risk of being dismissed from the Quakers for breaking their tenets. Still, she supported independence. The British were aware of her feelings, but knowing her religion, they were not threatened by her. Darragh herself would tell them, "Though we consider thee as a public enemy, we regard thee as a private friend. While we detest the cause thee fights for, we wish well to thy personal interest and safety."[2]

In December 1777, Darragh found herself involved in the war nevertheless. Her house was across the street from a building being used by General William Howe as his headquarters, and she was often visited by a British officer, Major John Andre. The major explained that Darragh's house would also be used by the British for private conferences.

Darragh had no choice but to let the British use the large back parlor of her home for their meetings. Darragh was told that a room in her house would be required that very evening and that she should prepare it for a meeting. Also, she was told that her family should go to sleep early so that they could not overhear anything that was discussed.

Darragh did as she was told. She prepared the room and sent her family to bed. She admitted the British into the house and assured them that everyone there was in bed except herself and that she would go directly there as soon as she had shown the officers to their meeting room.

However, Darragh was in a quandary. While she had publicly supported the patriot cause, she had never acted on her beliefs. Still, her family

Under British rule, Americans were often forced to provide room
and board in their own homes for British soldiers. After America
gained independence, the Third Amendment was written to prohibit
soldiers from lodging at private residences unless given permission
by the owner.

was so committed to the cause of independence that Darragh's son Charles was serving in the Second Pennsylvania Regiment at Whitemarsh even though his actions now separated him from the religion in which he had been raised. Darragh and her husband are not known to have objected to his service, though it must have pained them to see their son cast off his religion.

Darragh was not sure what she alone should do to support the war effort and protect her son's life. Her religion forbade her from becoming involved, but many soldiers' lives were at risk, including her son's. After a short time of nervous debate and a great deal of prayer, she got up, crept down the corridor, and eavesdropped on the British meeting.

At first, the murmurs of the men speaking were too quiet for her to hear through the door. Perhaps she even thought of going back to her bed. But soon a stronger voice spoke out, reading an order for troops to march from Philadelphia on December 4 in order to ambush General George Washington's forces at Valley Forge and Whitemarsh.

Darragh went back to bed. Soon she heard someone knocking on her door, but she did not answer. The person knocked a second time, more loudly, but still Darragh lay in bed without answering. Finally, after the third knock, this one very loud, Darragh rose and answered the door. She escorted Major Andre and the others out of her house and went back to bed, but did not sleep.

During her sleepless night, Darragh formulated a plan to warn Washington's troops. She was required to get a pass to leave the city, but she knew a way she could acquire one that would not raise suspicion. Early on the morning of December 3, Darragh went to Howe's headquarters and requested permission to get flour at a mill in the town of Frankford. Her request was not an unusual one and was granted as a matter of course.

Darragh took an empty flour sack and walked several miles through the snow until she found a member of the Pennsylvania militia. He was Lieutenant Colonel Thomas Craig, a friend of the family. She passed on the information she had heard and was assured by Craig that he would get the news to General Washington immediately. Darragh made him promise not to reveal who had given him the news, as the British would punish her and her family if they found out. Craig promised and left for Washington's headquarters. Darragh then went to

The drawing above shows Lydia Darragh warning an American soldier
of impending British attacks. According to some historians, Darragh was
also successful at sending information about the British by more
secretive methods. After listening to conversations by British soldiers,
she sewed tiny notes under the cloth covering of her son's coat buttons,
which he would then wear to see his brother, a lieutenant in the
American army.

A portrait of Major John Andre. Andre's memoirs of his time in the American colonies are some of the most trusted sources of the Revolutionary War from the British perspective. Andre acted as a spy for the British and was eventually caught by the Americans and hanged in 1780.

get the flour and returned home as if nothing unusual had happened.

Darragh was in a state of agitation as the British left Philadelphia for their planned ambush. But because of her warning, Washington was aware of the attack, and it was foiled. Darragh learned of this when Major Andre returned to question her about her family and whether any of them were awake the night of the meeting. Darragh insisted she had sent everyone to bed early. Major Andre was said to have replied, "You, Lydia, I know, were asleep; I had to knock on your door three times before you heard me. Yet it is certain we were betrayed. I am altogether at a loss to conceive who could have given information of our intended attack to General Washington."[3]

The officer left, and Darragh breathed a sigh of relief. Craig kept his word and during the war, no one ever knew what Darragh had done. Her daughter Ann, however, told the story of her mother's courage years after the war was over and the danger had passed. Lydia Darragh died in Philadelphia at sixty years of age in 1789.

MERCY OTIS WARREN

Mercy Otis Warren was born on September 25, 1728, in Barnstable, Massachusetts, to an upper-class family. Her family had come to the colonies in 1630 and had lived in the Plymouth area ever since. Warren herself never left the area of eastern Massachusetts, but through her plays and her correspondence, she was one of the more influential women's voices during the Revolution.

The Otis family was involved in politics, and Mercy listened with interest to the conversations between her father and her brother James. Although her brothers were sent to Harvard, she, like other women of her time, was limited to the education she was able to obtain for herself, although her parents did encourage her to read extensively. Still, she was bitterly resentful that she was relegated to performing hours upon hours of needlework while the men in the family learned Latin and Greek and engaged in public discourse on political events.

The men in her family did not limit their involvement to mere debate on the issues, however. Mercy's brother James was so eager to spread the fever of independence that he had quarreled with a British officer in 1769 and received a brutal blow to his head.

This is a portrait of Mercy Otis Warren. Besides her plays and histories, Warren also wrote poetry. A collection entitled *Poems, Dramatic and Miscellaneous*, written in 1790, was the first of her writings to be published under her real name. She was in her early sixties when the work was published.

After that, he experienced occasional bouts of illness
until his death in 1783, though he continued to
espouse the patriot cause and served in the war.

At twenty-six years of age, Mercy Otis married
James Warren, who was also avidly interested in
politics. He encouraged his wife's active involvement and supported her in her efforts. The
Warrens eventually had five sons.

Warren's political interests inspired her to
turn to writing. In the years before the
Revolutionary War, she wrote several plays: *The
Adulateur* (1772), *The Defeat* (1773), and *The Group*
(1775). In her plays, she skewered the British
overlords of the colonies with her finely tuned
sarcastic wit. The governor of Massachusetts, for
example, was portrayed as Rapatio, a monster
intent on raping the colony for the crown. Warren
was not afraid to direct her attacks at well-known
public officials, though in the beginning her
works were published anonymously. In puritanical
New England, the job of playwright was considered a vulgar occupation, hardly fit for a man and
certainly not for a woman. Acting and writing
plays was frowned upon throughout the colonies.
The theater was not held in high repute as a cultural institution until well into the nineteenth

century. Writing anonymously assured Warren that her work would be read and not dismissed outright because of her gender.

However, Warren could not completely escape the clutches of the culture in which she had grown up. Even though she had great talent and the support of her family, she still had nagging doubts about performing such unfeminine tasks. Her correspondence shows she often solicited the advice of friends on whether she was living her life appropriately. In a letter to John Adams, she asked if he thought her "deficient" in womanly attributes if she parodied Thomas Hutchinson, the governor of Massachusetts and a supporter of the Stamp Act, along with his political allies, in a new play. At the time, Adams supported Warren's desire to embrace the patriot cause through her plays and pamphlets, although in later years when he himself was the subject of her sarcastic wit, he altered his opinion on the suitability of female writers.

The ambiguity surrounding a woman who was a wife and mother as well as a political activist was represented by Warren's own husband, who referred to her as having a "masculine genius."[1] In other words, while he supported her efforts, he still felt her choice of vocation was unique within

Above is a painting of the Battle of Bunker Hill by American artist John Trumbull. Although the Americans lost the battle, they were able to weaken the British army, which lost more than 1,000 soldiers in combat. The outcome strengthened American resolve and proved that the British army could be overcome in time.

the realm of what was then considered acceptable feminine behavior.

Warren's husband served as a soldier during the war and often wrote descriptions of the battles he had witnessed in letters to his wife. In describing the Battle of Bunker Hill, in a letter dated June 18, 1775, he wrote, "It is Impossible to describe the Confusion in this place, Women & Children flying into the Country, armed Men Going to the field,

and wounded Men returning from there fill the
Streets. I shant Attempt a description—your Brother
borrowed a Gun [and] went among the flying
Bullets . . ."[2] Besides keeping informed of what was
happening in the war, Warren supported the cause
through her writing. She wrote to those people she
knew were suffering due to the consequences of
the war—not just her friends and acquaintances—
but to anyone. When Warren learned of the death
of General Richard Montgomery in January 1776,
she wrote to his widow.

> While you are deriving comfort from the
> Highest Source, it may still brighten the
> clouded moment to reflect that the number
> of your friends is not confined to the
> narrow limits of the province but by the
> happy union of the American Colonies . . .
> and the urn of the companion of your
> heart will be sprinkled with the tears of
> thousands who revere the commander at
> the gates of Quebec, though not personally
> acquainted with the General.[3]

Warren maintained correspondence with many
of the important political figures of her day, including Samuel Adams, John Adams, and Thomas
Jefferson. She was also a lifelong correspondent of

A letter from General George Washington to Mercy Otis Warren, dated November 4, 1790. In the letter, Washington praises some of her writing, which she sent to him for review.

John Adams's wife, Abigail. Abigail Adams once wrote to Warren:

> You, Madam, are so sincere a lover of your country, and so hearty a mourner in all her misfortunes, that it will greatly aggravate your anxiety to hear how much she is now oppressed and insulted. To you, who has so thoroughly looked through the deeds of men, no action, however base or sordid, no measure, however cruel and villainous, will be a matter for any surprise.[4]

To Warren, who wrote of the plight of the colonies with such passion, her opinions and actions were not heroic, but instinctive. She wrote:

> The late convulsions are only the natural struggle which ensued when the genius of liberty arises to assert her rights in opposition to the ghost of tyranny. I doubt not this fell form will ere long be driven from our land. Then may the western skies behold virtue, which is generally the attendant of freedom. Seated on the throne of peace, where may she ever preside over the rising commonwealth of America.[5]

Oppression in the American colonies was not the only political issue addressed in Warren's works. In her play *The Group*, she argued that

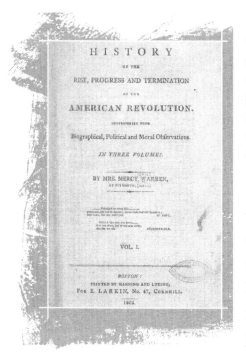

This is the original title page of Warren's exhaustive three-volume history of the American Revolution, published in 1805. Even today it is acknowledged to be one of the earliest and most accurate accounts of the war.

women should have the right to be liberated from abusive husbands. Later, in a nineteen-page pamphlet, she opposed the ratification of the U.S. Constitution because it did not yet have a bill of rights, it did not provide term limits for elected officials, and it provided no safeguard against the federal government raising a standing army.

During the war, Warren began a history of the Revolution, which eventually became a work entitled *The History of the Rise and Progress and Termination of the American Revolution*. It was published in 1805 when Warren was seventy-seven years old. Warren was no longer satisfied with being anonymous; her three-volume history was published with her name proudly displayed upon it. Because of this, Warren is often considered the first true U.S.

A statue of Mercy Otis Warren was placed in front of the Barnstable County Superior Courthouse to honor her patriotism and literary contributions. The statue was dedicated in 2001. It stands near a statue of her brother, James Otis.

woman author. Other women were writing at the same time, and a few others were published, but normally, women did not expect their work to find publication. Warren was the first woman in the country who wrote with the goal of having her work published and distributed widely.

Mercy Otis Warren died in 1814. In her honor, a bronze statue was dedicated at the courthouse in Barnstable, Massachusetts, on July 4, 2001. It stands opposite a statue of another Barnstable patriot hero, her brother James Otis.

ESTHER DEBERDT REED

One of the staunchest supporters of American independence had been raised in England to be loyal to the British Crown. Esther DeBerdt Reed was born in London in 1746, the only daughter of Dennis DeBerdt, a successful merchant whose main business was with the American colonies. Due to the nature of DeBerdt's pursuits, many of his American clients and business partners visited the DeBerdt residence in London. One of them, Joseph Reed, wooed the young Esther. Eventually, they were engaged.

Esther Reed and her husband, Joseph, shared a mutual love for America and a passionate determination to see it freed from British rule. Esther's parents agreed to their marriage on condition that the pair remained in London. However, Joseph's business affairs required the couple to take up residence in America.

However, Esther's father disapproved of the match, at least until such time as Joseph Reed had established himself in business. By 1765, Reed had returned to Philadelphia to begin his quest for a stable career and income. At first, his law practice went well, but when business eventually deteriorated, the engagement of Esther and Joseph stretched for five long years.

Esther, though raised to be politically loyal to Great Britain, had been exposed to too many ideas from the colonies to quietly accept that they should tamely submit to British domination. She wrote in one letter that she detested Prime Minister Grenville and Alexander Wedderburn because "they are such enemies to America."[1] To Joseph she wrote, " I could not think of letting this Express go without Congratulating you on the repeals of the Stamp Act."[2]

In 1769, Joseph Reed returned to Great Britain to find his fiancée's family beset by bankruptcy and grief over Dennis DeBerdt's death. The young couple were married in May 1770. In October of that same year, Joseph Reed returned to Philadelphia with his British bride.

When the war broke out, Joseph joined the army, leaving his wife at home to work the farm and raise their two children. Esther wrote to her brother Dennis in 1775 of her staunch support for the patriot cause: "I imagine we shall declare for independence, and exert our utmost to defend ourselves. This proposition would have alarmed almost every person on the Continent a twelve-month ago, but now the general voice is, if the Ministry and Nation will drive us to it, we must do it, rather than submit, after so many public resolutions to the contrary."[3] Her letters show that at this same time, Reed was also unsure of herself, while still maintaining the proper role of a woman subservient to her husband. She wrote in 1777, "As I am not famous for making good Bargains in things out of my Sphere I shall put it off as long as possible, in hopes you may be at home before it is too late."[4]

However, like many other women in the colonies, Reed learned to manage without a spouse. As a result, she became much more self-reliant and confident in her abilities. Several times during the war, Reed was forced to move her family to escape the approach of British forces. They moved first to Burlington, Vermont, and then to Evesham, New Jersey, where an aged relative and a female friend joined Reed and her children. While in Evesham, Reed was in poor health due to the recent birth of her third child. The family later moved to Flemington, New Jersey, where they remained until after the British withdrawal from Philadelphia in 1778.

One of Reed's children died of smallpox that year, and she wrote, "Calamity has over come me, and struck the very bottom of my heart."[5]

Shortly thereafter, the family returned to their home in Philadelphia. Joseph Reed had been elected governor of the state, and the family enjoyed high status and acclaim for both Reed's endurance of hardship and her husband's new position.

In 1780, Reed gave birth to another child, a son named George Washington Reed. Although ill again from the effects of childbirth, Reed gallantly contributed her time and effort to a new project of hers she initiated: the Ladies' Association.

On June 10, 1780, thirty-three-year-old Reed published a pamphlet entitled "The Sentiments of an American Woman." In the pamphlet, she declared that American women would not be content to simply wait at home for the men to determine the outcome of the war. Because getting women actively engaged in the war effort meant deliberately crossing gender lines, Reed composed her arguments in such a way that womens' involvement would seem patriotic rather than scandalous. She listed famous heroines of the past like Joan of Arc, who had fought "the ancestors of these same British, whose odious yoke we have just shaken off, and whom it is necessary that we drive from this Continent."[6]

THE SENTIMENTS of an
AMERICAN WOMAN.

ON the commencement of actual war, the Women of America manifested a firm resolution to contribute as much as could depend on them, to the deliverance of their country. Animated by the purest patriotism, they are fensible of forrow at this day, in not offering more than barren wifhes for the fuccefs of fo glorious a Revolution. They afpire to render themfelves more really ufeful; and this fentiment is univerfal from the north to the fouth of the Thirteen United States. Our ambition is kindled by the fame of thofe heroines of antiquity, who have rendered their fex illuftrious, and have proved to the univerfe, that, if the weaknefs of our Conftitution, if opinion and manners did not forbid us to march to glory by the fame paths as the Men, we fhould at leaft equal, and fometimes furpafs them in our love for the public good. I glory in all that which my fex has done great and commendable. I call to mind with enthufiafm and with admiration, all thofe acts of courage, of conftancy and patriotifm, which hiftory has tranfmitted to us: The people favoured by Heaven, preferved from deftruction by the virtues, the zeal and the refolution of Deborah, of Judith, of Efther! The fortitude of the mother of the Macchabees, in giving up her fons to die before her eyes: Rome faved from the fury of a victorious enemy by the efforts of Volumnia; and other Roman Ladies: So many famous fieges where the Women have been feen forgetting the weaknefs of their fex, building new walls, digging trenches with their feeble hands; furnifhing arms to their defenders, they themfelves darting the miffile weapons on the enemy, refigning the ornaments of their apparel, and their fortune, to fill the public treafury; and to haften the deliverance of their country; burying themfelves under its ruins; throwing themfelves into the flames rather than fubmit to the difgrace of humiliation before a proud enemy.

Born for liberty, difdaining to bear the irons of a tyrannic Government, we affociate ourfelves to the grandeur of thofe Sovereigns, cherifhed and revered, who have held with fo much fplendour the fcepter of the greateft States, The Batildas, the Elizabeths, the Maries, the Catharines, who have extended the empire of liberty, and contented to reign by fweetnefs and juftice, have broken the chains of flavery, forged by tyrants in the times of ignorance and barbarity. The Spanifh Women, do they not make, at this moment, the moft patriotic facrifices, to encreafe the means of victory in the hands of their Sovereign. He is a friend to the French Nation. They are our allies. We call to mind, doubly interefted, that it was a French Maid who kindled up amongft her fellow-citizens, the flame of patriotifm buried under long misfortunes: It was the Maid of Orleans who drove from the kingdom of France the anceftors of thofe fame Britifh, whofe odious yoke we have juft fhaken off; and whom it is neceffary that we drive from this Continent.

But I muft limit myfelf to the recollection of this fmall number of atchievements. Who knows if perfons difpofed to cenfure, and fometimes too feverely with regard to us, may not difapprove our appearing acquainted even with the actions of which our fex boafts? We are at leaft certain, that he cannot be a good citizen who will not applaud our efforts for the relief of the armies which defend our lives, our poffeffions, our liberty? The fituation of our foldiery has been reprefented to me; the evils infeparable from war, and the firm and generous fpirit which has enabled them to fupport thefe. But it has been faid, that they may apprehend, that, in the courfe of a long war, the view of their diftreffes may be loft, and their fervices be forgotten. Forgotten! never; I can anfwer in the name of all my fex. Brave Americans, your difinterestedness, your courage, and your conftancy will always be dear to America, as long as fhe fhall preferve her virtue.

Esther Reed's pamphlet, "The Sentiments of an American Woman," spurred the creation of the Ladies' Association of Philadelphia, the first women's organization in America.

Reed admitted in the pamphlet that there would be those who disapproved of her endeavors, but she insisted that a true patriot would "applaud our efforts for the relief of the armies which defend our lives, our possessions, our liberty."[7] By depicting those who would bar women's involvement in the war as unpatriotic, Reed won many sympathizers. Only three days after the publication of the pamphlet, thirty-six Philadelphia women met to decide how they could best focus their efforts.

The group was to begin a fund-raiser. The women were determined to send all contributions to Martha Washington for direct disbursement to the troops. The plan required an enormous amount of organization because the women wanted to cover all thirteen colonies. Their plan called for each colony's efforts to be supervised by a "Treasuress" and for these women in turn to be supervised by the wife of the governor of that colony. Reed, as the wife of Pennsylvania's governor, was responsible for approaching the wives of the other governors.

The Philadelphia group immediately set out by dividing the city into ten equal districts and assigning women to canvass each district. The

women traveled in pairs and were instructed to
visit every house without exception. Many
prominent women of the day participated in the
canvassing, including Sarah Franklin Bache, the
daughter of Benjamin Franklin.

Normally, women of such social standing at
that time would not dream of soliciting people of
all classes, including strangers, and asking them
for contributions. But the women approached the
canvassing with the fervor associated with their
zeal for independence. One of the participants
wrote anonymously, "those who were in the
country returned without delay to the city to fulfil
their duty."[8]

The women were received well by most people,
less well by some. The anonymous letter writer
continued, "as the cause of their visit was known,
they were received with all the respect due to so
honorable a commission."[9] On the other hand, Anne
Rawle's description of the women is less compli-
mentary: "Of all absurdities the Ladies going about
for money exceeded everything."[10] Rawle was
writing her mother, Rebecca Shoemaker, whose second husband was an exiled British sympathizer. She
continued, "I fancy they raised a considerable sum
by this extorted contribution."[11]

Overall, the Ladies' Association canvassers were greeted warmly, and many people contributed to their cause. By early July, the women had collected more than $300,000 in continental dollars. (Due to inflation, this was worth only about $7,500 in gold.) Still, it was a worthy sum and the women were duly proud of their efforts.

The distribution of the money collected by the Ladies' Association was hampered not by the citizens of Philadelphia but rather by George Washington himself. The general felt the money should not be disbursed directly to the troops. He told the Ladies' Association that the soldiers were in need of linen shirts. Reed, disappointed that Washington had taken their successful effort and translated it into mere women's work, like sewing, wrote Washington again asking for permission to send cash to the soldiers. Washington again refused her request. Reed's husband wrote her, "The General is so decided that you have no Choice left so that the sooner you finish the Business the better."[12]

Reed realized she would have to fulfill Washington's request or all the efforts of the association would be wasted. The Philadelphia Ladies' Association made more than 2,000 shirts,

At the request of George Washington, the members of the Ladies' Association of Philadelphia made shirts for American soldiers. After Esther Reed died, the effort continued. One member sent a note with the newly made items that requested the soldiers wear the shirts with as much pleasure as they were made.

each embroidered with the name of the woman who made it. Unfortunately, Reed did not live to see the project to completion. She died that fall of dysentery, which was sweeping through Philadelphia. The administration of the Ladies' Association fell to Sarah Franklin Bache.

The women were thanked by George Washington when their work was completed. By relegating such ardent supporters of independence to the level of mere seamstresses, the Ladies'

Association and the funding drive begun by Reed has, somewhat unfairly, been characterized by some historians as "George Washington's Sewing Circle." Yet more groups soon took up the call thanks to Esther DeBerdt Reed's idea, and several other colonies formed organizations that contributed greatly to the war effort.

ELIZABETH MARTIN

6

Elizabeth Martin was born in Virginia. She and her husband, Abram, moved to South Carolina, where they lived in an area that, despite its small population, sent a large number of its sons to war to fight for independence. Martin herself had nine children, seven of them boys old enough to serve in the army. All seven enlisted, with their mother's enthusiastic support. A younger son remained at home, and Martin's only daughter married Captain

Edmund Wade of Virginia, who died in 1775 during the siege of Quebec.

Legend tells of a British officer who asked Martin how many sons she had, and when she answered that she had eight, seven in the Continental army, he sneered and told her "Really, Madam, you have enough of them." Martin is said to have replied, "No, sir, I wish I had fifty."[1] The advice Elizabeth Martin gave her sons was more like that given by a sergeant than a mother, "Go, boys, fight for your country. Fight till death, if you must, but never let your country be dishonored. Were I a man, I would go with you."[2]

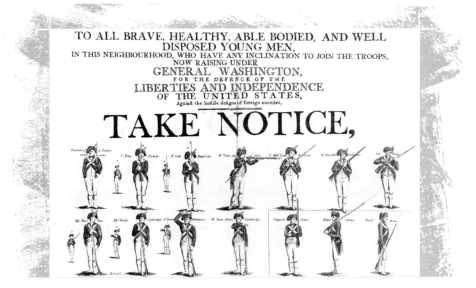

This hand-carved woodcut was a typical recruiting poster for the Continental army under General George Washington.

Another story tells of a British officer who cruelly told Martin that he had witnessed one of her sons die on the battlefield with his brains blown out of his head. Instead of collapsing into fits of weeping or hysterics at this grisly description, as the officer apparently hoped, Martin kept her composure and replied, "He could not have died in a nobler cause."[3]

Rachel Martin and Grace Martin, the wives of Martin's two oldest sons, shared this strong patriotism with their mother-in-law. One night, they were given a chance to do their part for their country. While they were at home, they received information that a British courier, accompanied by two guards, would be coming along the road that night, carrying dispatches for British posts. Rachel and Grace devised a plan to capture the dispatches.

Both woman changed into clothing taken from their husbands' closets, armed themselves, and then went to a point in the road where they knew the courier would pass. As the courier and his two guards approached their hiding spot, the two women jumped out of the darkness and aimed their pistols at the three men. Taken completely by surprise, the men immediately surrendered. Rachel and Grace took the dispatches from the courier and disappeared back

Rachel and Grace Martin, pictured in this undated illustration, disguised themselves in men's attire to support the Patriot cause. During the Revolutionary War, many women pretended to be British loyalists in order to gain valuable information about British attack plans or troop movements. Among their many strategies included eavesdropping on conversations or intercepting British soldiers bearing dispatches.

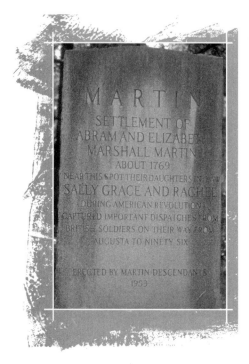

Descendants of the Martin family erected this gravestone in 1953 in order to commemorate the family's heroic involvement in the American Revolutionary War. Along with the names of Grace and Rachel Martin, the stone lists all the Martin boys who served in the Continental Army: William, James, John, George, Barclay, Edmund, Marshall, and Matthew.

into the darkness. Once they arrived home, they asked a trusted friend to take the messages to General Nathanael Greene.

The three men the women had waylaid now had no reason to continue on toward the British posts. They instead returned down the road, back past the Martin household. The men stopped there and asked for accommodations for the night. Elizabeth Martin asked them why they were back so soon after having passed the other way, and they replied they had been ambushed and relieved of their important papers by two young rebels.

The three were accepted into the house, never knowing that they slept under the same roof as the "men" who had taken them prisoner.

SYBIL LUDINGTON

"The British are burning Danbury—muster at Ludington's!"[1]

Two years after Paul Revere's famous midnight ride, a sixteen-year-old farm girl rode 40 miles (64 km) through the night to alert the militia of Fredericksburg, New York (present-day Ludingtonville), to danger.

Born in 1761 to Colonel Henry Ludington, a well-known and respected militia officer, and his wife, Abigail, Sybil Ludington was

Paul Revere (1735–1818), pictured in this engraving, was a prominent silversmith who is best remembered for his "midnight ride" to Lexington, Massachusetts, on April 19, 1775. Like Ludington, Revere spread the word about British troop movements in New England during the Revolutionary War. He was commemorated in the poem "Paul Revere's Ride" by Henry Wadsworth Longfellow in 1860.

the oldest of twelve children. As with other girls who had younger siblings, most of Ludington's time was spent doing household chores and caring for her brothers and sisters when her mother was occupied with her own tasks.

Ludington was just putting the younger children to bed on the night of April 26, 1777, when a messenger reached their house with the news that the British were burning the town of

Danbury, Connecticut, 17 miles (27 km) away. The messenger had come from Danbury's militia with a request for aid from Fredericksburg. The Danbury militia's food stores and munitions had been destroyed by the British, and the militia needed men, ammunition, food, and supplies to continue the fight.

It was going to be difficult to assemble the Fredericksburg militia quickly because all the men had temporarily been relieved of duty so they could see to the spring planting on their farms. Yet everyone would have to be alerted if aid was to be sent to Danbury. Colonel Ludington himself could not go; he would have to remain at his house to supervise the muster. Nor could the messenger from Danbury go; not only was he exhausted from his journey, but he was unfamiliar with the Fredericksburg area. He would not be able to find each farmhouse that would need to be alerted. Sybil Ludington, however, knew where the militia-men lived who had the responsibility of warning their area if danger arose. Ludington needed only to visit these houses for the word to then spread to everyone in the community.

Ludington was eager to rouse her neighbors for the defense of Danbury. Even though it was dark and raining, she had no doubt that she could

Sybil Ludington is pictured on her horse, Star, in this dynamic sculpture created by Anna Vaughn Hyatt Huntington in 1960. The sculpture is located in Carmel, New York, along Ludington's historic route.

find her way. Her father reluctantly agreed to let her go. After warning her to beware of British soldiers as well as "skinners," Henry Ludington sent his daughter off. Skinners were lawless men who used the chaos surrounding the war to make themselves rich by stealing. They had no allegiance to either the American or British side, although sometimes they dressed in uniforms as a disguise.

Although she failed to warn the residents of Danbury, Connecticut, before the arrival of British troops, Sybil Ludington is remembered for her courage and bravery during the American Revolution. This marker, which recounts her heroic ride, is located below another sculpture of her by Anna Vaughn Hyatt Huntington, at the library in Danbury.

Ludington promised her father she would be careful. She departed her home around 9 PM and traveled nearly 40 miles (64 km). She rode far and wide throughout the county, from the town of Kent, south to Mahopac, and north to Stormville, telling the men of the area of the need in Danbury. By the time Ludington and her horse returned home at dawn, wet and exhausted, nearly 400 men had departed to Danbury to fight the British.

Danbury lay in ruins; the Fredericksburg militia was organized too late to save it. But the militia was able to engage the British at the Battle of Ridgefield the following day on April 27, stopping the British advance. Before it reached Putnam County, New York, where the Ludingtons lived, the British retreated from Ridgefield and went back to their ships, which were anchored in Long Island Sound. Ludington's bravery may not have saved Danbury, but it did result in the British halting their advance through New England.

After the war, Ludington married Edmond Ogden, and the couple settled in the town of Catskill. Ludington had one son, Henry. Her husband died when Henry was only thirteen years old, so Ludington was forced to raise Henry alone. She supported herself and her child by working as a tavern keeper. Henry eventually became a lawyer, and his son graduated from West Point and became a military hero in his own right. There is a monument dedicated to him at Fort Riley in Kansas.

Sybil Ludington died in 1839 at her son's home in Unadilla, New York. Today, there is a trail dedicated to Ludington's route through Putnam County, New York. It is designated by markers for those who wish to retrace the path the sixteen-year-old took during the night of April 26, 1777. Ludington's ride was also commemorated on a U.S. postage stamp in 1975.

MARGARET CORBIN

Margaret Cochran Corbin was born in November 1751, near Chambersburg, Pennsylvania. At the age of five, she was orphaned when her parents were both killed during a Native American raid. Relatives raised Margaret and her siblings.

In 1772, Margaret married John Corbin. When he enlisted in the First Company of Pennsylvania Artillery, Margaret refused to be left behind. As was the case with many war wives, she had nothing to stay behind for, and so she became what is known as a camp follower. During the Revolutionary War, camp followers were the wives of the soldiers who followed the army and performed services like cooking food, laundering clothing, mending clothes, and tending to the wounded.

Life for camp followers was difficult. Just like the soldiers, they lived in extremely poor conditions through hot summers and freezing winters. They were not strangers to hunger and exhaustion. While recognizing that the women performed labor essential to the survival of the army, the army commanders had a tendency to dismiss them as a nuisance. The women received only a half-ration of the food allotted to the men. In one case, though, the laundresses of General Anthony Wayne's regiment waged a working strike until they were guaranteed better pay and living conditions. But even slightly improved circumstances could not keep the life of the camp followers from being hard and miserable.

Corbin made herself popular with the men in her husband's battery, and they affectionately called her Molly, a nickname she used for the rest of her life. The men even taught her how to clean and load a cannon, a task she learned quickly.

The actresses in this photograph are performing a typical task of camp followers in the Revolutionary War—mending uniforms. Camp followers were often soldiers' wives. They followed the troops from camp to camp and carried water, prepared meals, laundered and mended clothing, and occasionally took up arms during battle.

In November 1776, the British occupied New York City. The Continental army largely fled the city, leaving 2,000 Pennsylvania, Virginia, and Maryland men at Fort Washington on Manhattan Island, one of them being John Corbin. George Washington felt the fort should be completely evacuated, but General Nathanael Greene argued that it should be defended. Washington eventually agreed to this, and supplies and ammunition were ferried across the river to the fort.

On November 16, the defenders of the fort were attacked by Hessian infantry. Hessians were professional soldiers from Germany who had been hired by the British to help them in the war. During the battle, John Corbin was struck and killed by enemy fire. Margaret ran to him, but there was nothing she could do. Immediately, she picked up the rammer, the stick used to ram a cannonball to the bottom of the barrel. By doing this, she performed the task that had been her husband's duty.

Soon Corbin herself was struck by enemy fire. She was wounded in the shoulder and jaw, and her left arm was almost severed from her body. She lay with the rest of the wounded and dead on the battlefield.

These actors are loading a cannon with a rammer during a Revolutionary War reenactment. Cannons were one of the most effective weapons of the Revolutionary War. They were used on open battlefields and could hurl iron balls, small grapeshot, or shells long distances.

The Hessians killed many of the wounded after the battle, but for some reason, they did not kill Corbin. Perhaps the soldier who first found her thought she was dead or perhaps he did not want to bayonet a woman. Eventually, the British took Corbin prisoner. But within a short time, they had handed her over to the Continental army.

Corbin was stuck in a straw-filled cart with others who were wounded during battle and taken to Philadelphia. The trip must have been excruciatingly painful. It seems unlikely that anyone could have survived injuries such as Corbin's without bleeding to death or dying of infection, but somehow she survived.

In June 1777, Congress approved the formation of the Invalid Regiment, which was composed of soldiers too disabled to fight

British troops are seen in this undated engraving marching through the streets of New York City in September 1776. By October 28 of that same year, the British had captured Manhattan Island and were using New York Harbor as a chief entry port for the British invasion.

At left, an illustration of Margaret Corbin, the notoriously outspoken veteran of the Revolutionary War. Celebrated for her bravery in stepping forward to fire a cannon after her husband was killed, Corbin was among the few women who were recognized by the early American government for wartime actions.

again. Corbin was enrolled in the regiment and remained on its rolls until it was disbanded in 1783.

In 1779, Corbin was awarded $30 by the state of Pennsylvania, "to relieve her present necessities due to her disabled condition caused by wounds received while she filled with distinguished bravery the post of her husband who was killed by her side serving a piece of artillery at Fort Washington."[1] Congress voted her a military pension of half her husband's pay for the rest of her life. This was the first time a woman had been granted a military pension by the United States.

Life did not get easier for Corbin or the people around her after the war. She never regained the use of her arm and could not work, and records indicate that she was unable to bathe or dress herself. She also had habits like smoking, drinking, and swearing, as well as a terrible temper. The ladies of the area snubbed Corbin due to her uncouth ways, so she spent most of her time at the local garrison, trading stories with the soldiers. Because she had so little money, the soldiers offered her their cast-off clothing, which meant Corbin could usually be found dressed as an artillery officer. She persuaded everyone to call her Captain Molly and even convinced the soldiers to salute her.

Corbin had caregivers who used her pension for her upkeep. But Congress was often slow in paying the money, which made her caretakers cross. In 1795, Quartermaster William Price complained, "I am at a loss what to do with Capt. Molly. She is such an offensive person that people are unwilling to take her in charge."[2]

Corbin died in 1800 at the age of forty-nine. She was originally buried above the Hudson River

This sculpture of Molly Pitcher (Mary Ludwig Hays McCauly, 1754–1832) is located in Carlisle, Pennsylvania. Like Margaret Corbin, Molly Pitcher became famous when she took over for her husband after he was no longer able to fire his cannon.

near Highland Falls, New York, but in 1926, the Daughters of the American Revolution located her overgrown grave and arranged for her reburial at West Point. She was reinterred with full military honors, a granite memorial, and a bronze plaque.

AFTER THE WAR

9

In 1776, Abigail Adams wrote to her husband, "If perticular care and attention is not paid to the Ladies, we are determined to foment a Rebelion, and will not hold ourselves bound by any Laws in which we have no voice, or Representation."[1]

Abigail Adams was determined to push the boundaries of what was considered acceptable behavior for women at the time. She was realistic enough, though, to acknowledge that things wouldn't change in her own lifetime.

The end of the war did not vastly improve the situation for colonial women, but some strides had been made. Women who had learned to run farms and businesses while the men were away fighting were not eager to return to merely doing housework and taking care of children. For women who had married the men their parents chose for them, especially for those who were unhappily married, forcing their daughters into arranged unions was no longer acceptable. Women who had gained an education through hard work and dogged determination were not inclined to allow their own daughters to grow up illiterate.

But it was not just the women who had changed. Some men's opinions about women had changed, too. For example, a New Englander, William

Abigail Adams (1744–1818), wife of American president John Adams and mother of President John Quincy Adams, is seen in this early portrait. She was self-educated, a supporter of the Revolution, an abolitionist, and an advocate for women's education.

Palfrey, once dismissed his wife's opinions and advice. Palfrey thought of his wife, Susan, as an extension of himself. When, in 1778, she wanted to move to Boston, a decision he opposed, he chided her in a letter, "Can you suppose that I can possibly have an Interest separate from yours?" He insisted that when it came to his family's best interests, "You cannot possibly be a Judge."[2] This condescending tone had changed only a year later after his wife had competently taken over the family's financial affairs. Palfrey began regularly consulting with his wife on financial matters, and before he sailed to France, he informed his wife of all the arrangements he had made concerning his estate.

Timothy Pickering also learned the value of a wife who was educated in conducting the family business. In June 1777, he sent a lame horse home, instructing his wife to ask his male friends for advice on how to care for it, because such a task was "entirely out of [your] sphere."[3] His letters continue in this tone for several years, but eventually Pickering changed his tune. While he was off fighting the war, his wife capably handled their farm, rented another farm, supervised the building of their new home, and got the harvest in, all while caring for a newborn infant. Pickering wrote in 1783, "This war which has so often [and] long separated us, has taught me how to value you."[4]

Lucy Knox wrote to her husband that when he came home from the war, "I hope you will not consider yourself as commander in chief of your own house—but be convinced . . . that there is such a thing as equal command."[5]

In love as well as business, things had changed on the home front. Young girls who had seen their mothers overcome obstacles to become successful in business and farming were not necessarily interested in either marrying young or in what their parents had to say about their choice of husband. The adults who had fought the war agreed with the sentiment. Thomas Jefferson declared in a letter to a French acquaintance in 1790, "According to the usage of my country, I scrupulously suppressed my wishes, that my daughter might indulge her own sentiments freely."[6] An anonymous New Englander declared in 1784, "In a matter of such importance, a young woman ought to [be] left [e]ntirely to herself."[7]

Even the previously dreaded title of spinster was no longer as spurned as it had been. Instead, women began to realize the value of choosing a life according to their own wishes, and whether that meant marriage. Spinsterhood came to be seen by some as "a situation that may be supported with great dignity."[8] In 1800, Eliza Southgate of Maine remarked, "I do not esteem marriage absolutely essential to happiness."[9]

While it was true that some marriages had become more egalitarian—some women had chosen to have fewer children by breastfeeding for a longer time, and others had lived on their own compared to before the war—by and large the situation for women remained little improved. The main change had come in the form of people's altered perception of what constituted the "female sphere." Raising children was still considered the highest feminine calling, but women's options would never again be as restricted as they had been. Journals such as *The Christian's, Scholar's and Farmer's Magazine* began to address its female readers' interests as well as the men's interests, assuming for the first time that women constituted a significant portion of its readership. The journal declared, "Conscious we are of the dignity, importance, and merit of the fair daughters of our country; and, with cheerfulness, we shall devote some portion of this work to their peculiar advantage and amusement."[10]

Perhaps the biggest alteration to society then was in the matter of education. Before the war, most women received no education, except perhaps some instruction on reading the Bible. If a girl wanted more schooling, she generally had to figure out a way to get it on her own, as in Deborah Samson's case when she borrowed the schoolbooks of others.

After the war, public schools were open to girls as well as boys. Private academies also began admitting female students. In these schools, girls learned history, geography, and mathematics alongside the boys. The early nineteenth century saw many female reformers emerge from this first generation of educated American women. The women of past generations encouraged their daughters, nieces, and friends to take advantage of these newfound opportunities. Abigail Adams wrote to a niece in 1785, "It is from feeling the disadvantages of it myself, that I am the more solicitous that my young acquaintance should excel me."[11]

The heroines of the Revolutionary War did more than simply perform one or two courageous

Male and female pupils are pictured in this undated illustration of a colonial schoolroom. While some individuals in eighteenth-century America believed women should be formally educated in order to raise literate children, others were opposed to this idea.

feats. Deborah Samson may have had to dress as a man to fight for her country, but eventually women would be able to serve in the armed forces without the need for disguise. Mercy Otis Warren may have felt forced to publish her plays anonymously for fear of attracting derision for entering an occupation intended only for men, but by the early nineteenth century, Warren and other women were putting their own names on their written work.

The war didn't change everything, but it did open a few doors for women. The woman who was supposed to be happy in a chimney corner raising children and being innocent of finances or farm work had become more knowledgeable, skilled, and independent. In 1798, Judith Sargent rather colorfully predicted that women had entered a new dawn of history. She said that women were "emerging from the clouds which have hitherto enveloped them, and the revolution of events is advancing in that half of the human species, which hath hitherto been involved in the night of darkness . . ."[12]

Women had a long way to go, but heroines like Deborah Samson, Lydia Darragh, Mercy Otis Warren, Mary Cochran Corbin, Nancy

This obelisk marks the Oriskany Battlefield in Whitestone, New York, a historic site of the Revolutionary War. The Battle of Oriskany took place on August 6, 1777, and marked an important American victory. Under General Nicholas Herkimer, the Continental army forced the British into Canada, which destroyed their campaign and led to the surrender of Saratoga, New York.

Morgan Hart, and countless others braved scorn, derision, and sometimes death to take the first few steps in a new direction for women in the United States.

TIMELINE

1754–1760	French and Indian War occurs.
1764	Sugar Act and Currency Act are passed by Parliament.
1765	Stamp Act is passed.
1766	Stamp Act is repealed.
1772	Mercy Otis Warren's *The Adulateur* is published.
1773	Mercy Otis Warren's *The Defeat* is published.
1775	Mercy Otis Warren's *The Group* is published.
April 1775	Revolutionary War begins after the Battles of Lexington and Concord.
June 1775	The Battle of Bunker Hill is fought outside Boston.
March 1776	The British leave Boston.
July 1776	The colonies declare their independence.
November 1776	Mary Cochran Corbin is wounded at Fort Washington.
April 1777	Sybil Ludington rides to muster the militia.
June 1777	The Invalid Regiment is formed and Mary Corbin is enrolled.
September 1777	The British capture Philadelphia.
December 1777	Lydia Darragh delivers her message to the army.
February 1778	France enters the war on the side of the United States.
October 1778	Deborah Samson enlists under the name Robert Shurtleff.

1779	Mary Corbin is awarded a military pension.
June 1779	The British leave Philadelphia.
1780	Esther DeBerdt Reed begins her fund drive.
1781	General Cornwallis surrenders at Yorktown, Virginia.
April 1783	The Treaty of Paris, which officially ends the war, is ratified by Congress.
1805	Congress grants Deborah Samson a veteran's pension; Mercy Otis Warren's three-volume history of the Revolutionary War is published.

Glossary

ambush A trap in which a concealed person lies in wait in order to attack another person by surprise.

bankruptcy The state of being impoverished.

boycott To purposefully refuse to have dealings with a person, store, or organization; to refuse the traded goods of a foreign country or countries.

canvasser A person who goes door-to-door throughout a district in order to solicit political support or to determine opinions.

Hessian A German soldier paid by the British to fight for them; a mercenary.

Loyalist An American who was loyal to the British cause; also called a Tory.

mercenary A soldier who is hired by a government to fight for it.

militia Local men who would gather when called to fight but were not enlisted in the army.

pension A fixed sum paid regularly to a person following his or her retirement from service.

Quartering Act A law that required the colonies to provide barracks and supplies to British troops.

skinner A thief who was not allied with either British or American forces.

For More Information

American Historical Association of Women and Minorities
400 A Street SE
Washington, DC 20003
(202) 544-2422

National Museum of Women's History
P.O. Box 1296
Annandale, VA 22003
(703) 813-6209
Web site: http://www.nmwh.org

National Women's Studies Association
University of Maryland
7100 Baltimore Boulevard
Suite 500
College Park, MD 20740
(301) 403-0525
Web site: http://www.nwsa.org

National Society of Daughters of the American Revolution
1776 D Street NW
Washington, DC 20006
(202) 628-1776
Web site: http://www.dar.org

Rare Manuscript and Book Collections
Duke University
Durham, NC 27708
(919) 684-8111
Web site: http://www.duke.edu

WEB SITES
Due to the changing nature of Internet links, the
Rosen Publishing Group, Inc., has developed an
online list of Web sites related to the subject of
this book. This site is updated regularly. Please
use this link to access the list:

http://www.rosenlinks.com/aww/wssp

For Further Reading

Cappon, Lester J., ed. *The Adams-Jefferson Letters: The Complete Correspondence Between Thomas Jefferson and Abigail and John Adams.* Chapel Hill, NC: University of North Carolina Press, 1988.

Diamant, Lincoln, ed. *Revolutionary Women in the War for American Independence: A One-Volume Revised Edition of Elizabeth Ellet's 1848 Landmark Series.* Westport, CT: Praeger Press, 1998.

Gunderson, Joan R. *To Be Useful to the World: Women in Revolutionary America, 1740–1790* (American Women, 1600–1900). New York: Twayne Publishers, 1996.

Hamilton, Alexander, et al. *The Federalist Papers.* Dublin, Ireland: Mentor Books, 1999.

Hoffman, Ronald, ed. *Women in the Age of the American Revolution* (Perspectives on the American Revolution). Charlottesville, VA: University of Virginia Press, 1989.

Martin, Joseph Plumb. *A Narrative of a Revolutionary Soldier.* New York: Signet Classic, 2001.

Norton, Mary Beth. *Liberty's Daughters: The Revolutionary Experience of American Women, 1750–1800.* Ithaca, NY: Cornell University Press, 1980.

Bibliography

"Amazing Women in War and Peace." Userpages.aug. com. Retrieved January 18, 2003 (http://userpages. aug.com/captbarb/femvets.html).

Bailyn, Bernard. *The Ideological Origins of the American Revolution.* Cambridge, MA: Belknap Press, 1992.

Clyne, Patricia Edwards. *Patriots in Petticoats.* New York: Dodd, Mead & Company, 1976.

Commager, Henry Steele, and Richard B. Morris, eds. *The Spirit of Seventy-Six: The Story of the American Revolution as Told by the Participants.* New York: De Capo Press, 1995.

Dacquino, V. T. "Sybil Ludington: The Call to Arms." Catskill.net. Retrieved February 10, 2003 (http://www.catskill.net/purple/sybil.htm).

"Declaration of Faith Issued by the Richmond Conference in 1887." Quakerinfo.com. Retrieved February 6, 2003 (http://www.quakerinfo.com/ rdf.shtml).

DePauw, Linda Grant. *Founding Mothers: Women in America in the Revolutionary Era.* Boston: Houghton Mifflin Company, 1975.

Diamant, Lincoln, ed. *Revolutionary Women in the War for American Independence: A One-Volume Revised Edition of Elizabeth Ellet's 1848 Landmark Series.* Westport, CT: Praeger Press, 1998.

"Document 7: Esther DeBerdt to Joseph Reed, 18 March 1766." Women and Social Movement in the United States, 1775–2000. Retrieved February 9, 2003 (http://womhist.binghamton. edu/amrev/doc7.htm).

"Document 10: Esther Reed to Dennis DeBerdt, 28 October 1775." Women and Social Movement in the United States, 1775–2000. Retrieved February 9, 2003 (http://womhist.binghamton.edu/amrev/doc10.htm).

"Esther DeBerdt Reed." The White House. Retrieved February 9, 2003 (http://www. whitehouse.gov/kids/dreamteam/estherreed. html).

"Grace and Rachel Martin." Women in the American Revolution. Retrieved January 22, 2003 (http://rims.k12.ca.us/women_american_ revolution/martin.html).

Hintzen, William. "Betty Zane, Lydia Boggs, and Molly Scott: The Gunpowder Exploits at Fort Henry." WVCulture.org. Retrieved February 10, 2003 (http://www.wvculture.org/history/ journal_wvh/wvh55-4.html).

"Intolerable Acts, The." USHistory.org. Retrieved February 5, 2003 (http://www.ushistory.org/ declaration/related/intolerable.htm).

"Lydia Darragh." Women in the American Revolution. Retrieved February 6, 2003 (http:// rims.k12.ca.us/women_american_revolution/ darragh.html).

"Letter from James Warren to Mercy Otis Warren." Massachusetts Historical Society. Retrieved February 5, 2003, (http://www.masshist.org/bh/warrenp1text.html).

"Lydia Barrington Darragh." Encyclopedia Britannica. Retrieved February 6, 2003 (http://search.eb.com/women/articles/Darragh_Lydia_Barrington.html).

"Lydia Darragh." USHistory.org. Retrieved February 6, 2003 (http://www.ushistory.org/march/bio/lydia.htm).

Maier, Pauline. *From Resistance to Revolution: Colonial Radicals and the Development of American Opposition to Britain, 1765–1776*. New York: Alfred A. Knopf, 1973.

"Margaret Cochran Corbin." Distinguished Women of Past and Present. Retrieved January 22, 2003 (http://www.distinguishedwomen.com/biographies/corbin.html).

"Margaret Corbin." Encyclopedia Britannica. Retrieved January 22, 2003 (http://search.eb.com/women/articles/Corbin_Margaret.html).

Martin, Joseph Plumb. *A Narrative of a Revolutionary Soldier*. New York: Signet Classic, 2001.

"Mercy Otis Warren." Massachusetts Historical Society. Retrieved February 5, 2003 (http://www.masshist.org/bh/mercybio.html).

"Nancy Morgan Hart." Georgia Women of Achievement. Retrieved February 5, 2003 (http://www.gawomen.org/honoress/long/hartn_long.htm).

"Nancy Morgan Hart." National Society of the
Daughters of the American Revolution.
Retrieved February 5, 2003 (http://www.
geocities.com/Heartland/Meadows/6651)."

"Nancy Morgan Hart Historical Park."
Georgiamagazine.com. Retrieved February 5, 2003
(http://www.georgiamagazine.com/counties/elbert/
n_hart.htm).

Norton, Mary Beth. *Liberty's Daughters: The
Revolutionary Experience of American Women,
1750–1800.* Ithaca, NY: Cornell University
Press, 1980.

"Overview of the Revolutionary War." The Patriot
Resource. Retrieved February 5, 2003 (http://
www.patriotresource.com/history/1763.html).

Pepiot, Margery. "Captain Molly." National Muzzle
Loading Rifle Association. Retrieved February 10,
2003 (http://www.muzzleblasts.com/Vol3No4/
Articles/MBO34-3.htm).

Powell, Jim. "William Penn, America's First Great
Champion for Liberty and Peace." Quaker.org.
Retrieved February 6, 2003 (http://www.quaker.
org/wmpenn.html).

Rosman, Joel. "Lydia Barrington Darragh, The
'Brave Quakeress' Who Saved the Revolution."
Retrieved February 6, 2003 (http://www2.
whidbey.com/jerod/lydiadarragh.htm).

"Stamp Act." The Patriot Resource. Retrieved
February 5, 2003 (http://www.patriotresource.
com/events/stamp.html).

"Sybil Ludington." Danbury Historical Society. Retrieved February 10, 2003 (http://www. danburyhistorical.org/Ludington.html).

"Sybil Ludington—Female Paul Revere." National Society of the Daughters of the American Revolution. Retrieved February 10, 2003 (http://www.geocities.com/Heartland/ Plains1789/sybil.html).

"Sybil Ludington." Patterson, New York Web site. Retrieved February 10, 2003 (http://www. pattersonny.org/SybilLudington.htm).

"Sybil Ludington." Encyclopedia Britannica. Retrieved February 10, 2003 (http://search. eb.com/women/articles/Ludington_Sybil.html).

"Tributes to Nancy Morgan Hart." National Society of the Daughters of the American Revolution. Retrieved February 5, 2003 (http://www.geocities. com/Heartland/Meadows/6651/photo/nhhwy.html).

"Valley Forge FAQs." USHistory.org. Retrieved February 11, 2003 (http://www.ushistory.org/ valleyforge/youasked/070.htm).

"Women of the Revolution." ColonialAncestors.com. Retrieved January 22, 2003 (http:// colonialancestors.com/revolutionary/women.htm).

"Women's Military History." Woment's Internet Information Network. Retrieved January 22, 2003 (http://www.undelete.org/military/timeline1.html).

Zeinert, Karen. *Those Remarkable Women of the American Revolution.* Brookfield, CT: Millbrook Press, 1996.

Source Notes

Introduction

1. Henry Steele Commager and Richard B. Morris, editors, *The Spirit of Seventy-Six: The Story of the American Revolution as Told by the Participants* (New York: De Capo Press, 1995), p. 13.
2. Bernard Bailyn, *The Ideological Origins of the American Revolution* (Cambridge, MA: Belknap Press, 1992), pp. 210–211.
3. Pauline Maier, *From Resistance to Revolution: Colonial Radicals and the Development of American Opposition to Britain, 1765–1776* (New York: Alfred A. Knopf, 1973), p. 62.
4. Ibid., p. 56.
5. Mary Beth Norton, *Liberty's Daughters 1750–1800* (Ithaca, NY: Cornell University Press, 1980), p. 4.
6. Ibid., p. 42.
7. Linda Grant DePauw, *Founding Mothers: Women in America in the Revolutionary Era* (Boston: Houghton Mifflin Company, 1975), p. 49.
8. Norton, p. 5.
9. Lincoln Diamant, editor, *Revolutionary Women in the War for American Independence: A One-Volume Revised Edition of Elizabeth Ellet's 1848 Landmark Series* (Westport, CT: Praeger Press, 1998), p. 26.

Chapter 1

1. Lincoln Diamant, editor, *Revolutionary Women in the War for American Independence: A One-Volume Revised Edition of Elizabeth Ellet's 1848 Landmark Series* (Westport, CT: Praeger Press, 1998), p. 35.
2. Joseph Plumb Martin, *A Narrative of a Revolutionary Soldier* (New York: Signet Classic, 2001), p. 33.

Chapter 2

1. Patricia Edwards Clyne, *Patriots in Petticoats* (New York: Dodd, Mead & Company, 1976), p. 43.
2. Lincoln Diamant, editor, *Revolutionary Women in the War for American Independence: A One-Volume Revised Edition of Elizabeth Ellet's 1848 Landmark Series* (Westport, CT: Praeger Press, 1998), p.190.
3. Ibid., p.188.
4. "Nancy Hart Historical Park," GeorgiaMagazine. com, retrieved February 5, 2003 (http://www. georgiamagazine.com).

Chapter 3

1. "Declaration of Faith Issued by the Richmond Conference in 1887," Quakerinfo.com, retrieved February 6, 2003 (http://www. quakerinfo.com/rdf.html).
2. Joel Rosman, "Lydia Barrington Darragh, the 'Brave Quakeress' Who Saved the Revolution," retrieved February 6, 2003 (http://www2. whidbey.com/jerod/lydiadarragh.htm).

3. Lincoln Diamant, editor, *Revolutionary Women in the War for American Independence: A One-Volume Revised Edition of Elizabeth Ellet's 1848 Landmark Series* (Westport, CT: Praeger Press, 1998), p. 115.

Chapter 4
1. Mary Beth Norton, *Liberty's Daughters 1750–1800* (Ithaca, NY: Cornell University Press, 1980), p. 121.
2. "Letter from James Warren to Mercy Otis Warren," Massachusetts Historical Society, retrieved February 5, 2003 (http://www.masshist. org/bh/warrenp1text.html).
3. Lincoln Diamant, editor, *Revolutionary Women in the War for American Independence: A One-Volume Revised Edition of Elizabeth Ellet's 1848 Landmark Series* (Westport, CT: Praeger Press, 1998), p. 47.
4. Ibid., p. 44.
5. Ibid., p. 46.

Chapter 5
1. Lincoln Diamant, editor, *Revolutionary Women in the War for American Independence: A One-Volume Revised Edition of Elizabeth Ellet's 1848 Landmark Series* (Westport, CT: Praeger Press, 1998), p. 96.
2. "Document 7: Esther DeBerdt to Joseph Reed, 18 March 1766," Women and Social Movements in the United States, 1775–2000. Retrieved February 9, 2003 (http://womhist.binghamton. edu/amrev/doc7.htm).

3. "Document 10: Esther Reed to Dennis Dieberdt, 28 October 1775," Women and Social Movements in the United States, 1775–2000. Retrieved February 9, 2003 (http://www. womhist.binghamton.edu/amrev/doc10.htm).
4. Mary Beth Norton, *Liberty's Daughters 1750–1800* (Ithaca, NY: Cornell University Press, 1980), p. 216.
5. Diamant, p. 98.
6. Norton, p. 179.
7. Ibid.
8. Ibid., p. 180.
9. Ibid.
10. Ibid.
11. Ibid.
12. Ibid., p. 186.

Chapter 6
1. Lincoln Diamant, editor, *Revolutionary Women in the War for American Independence: A One-Volume Revised Edition of Elizabeth Ellet's 1848 Landmark Series* (Westport, CT: Praeger Press, 1998), p. 174.
2. Ibid.
3. "Women of the Revolution," Colonial Ancestors.com, retrieved January 22, 2003 (http://colonialancestors.com/revolutionary/women.htm).

Chapter 7

1. "Sybil Ludington," Danbury Historical Society, retrieved February 10, 2003 (http://www. danburyhistorical.org/Ludington.html).

Chapter 8

1. Margery Pepiot, "Captain Molly," National Muzzle Loading Rifle Association, retrieved February 10, 2003 (http://www.muzzleblasts. com/Vol3No4/Articles/MBO34-3.htm).
2. Ibid.

Chapter 9

1. Mary Beth Norton, *Liberty's Daughters 1750–1800* (Ithaca, NY: Cornell University Press, 1980), p. 226.
2. Ibid., p. 220.
3. Ibid., p. 221.
4. Ibid., p. 222.
5. Ibid., p. 224.
6. Ibid., p. 229.
7. Ibid.
8. Ibid., p. 240.
9. Ibid., p. 242.
10. Ibid., p. 246.
11. Ibid., p. 263.
12. Ibid., p. 295.

Index

About the Author

Martha Kneib is a native St. Louisian who holds a master's degree in anthropology. She devotes most of her time to writing, maintaining her Web sites, and traveling with her husband. This is her fourth book for the Rosen Publishing Group.

Photo Credits

Front cover, pp. 6, 79 Hulton Archive/Getty Images; back cover © Nancy Carter/North Wind Pictures; pp. 17, 25, 63, 68, 82 © North Wind Pictures Archives; pp. 9, 14, 20, 27, 31, 34, 37, 38, 41, 44, 52 (left and right), 60, 65, 90 Culver Pictures; p. 46 Library of Congress, Manuscript Division; pp. 48, 56 Library of Congress, Rare Book and Special Collections Division; p. 49 Mercy Otis Warren Committee, Barnstable, MA, David Lewis, sculptor; p. 66 courtesy of the Sumter National Forest; pp. 70, 71 © Matthew Weber; pp. 76, 78 © Carl & Ann Purcell/Corbis; p. 80 © West Point Museum Art Collection, United States Military Academy; p. 85 courtesy of the Massachusetts Historical Society; p. 92 © Lee Snider/Corbis.

Designer: Evelyn Horovicz; **Editor:** Joann Jovinelly; **Photo Researcher:** Peter Tomlinson